GUITAR *Listen & Learn*
HOMESPUN MUSIC INSTRUCTION

T0059261

TRAUM
TEACHES
Essential Blues for Acoustic Guitar

Recorded and mixed by Tom Mark
at Make Believe Ballroom, Shokan, NY.

Front and Back cover photos by Adam Traum.

ISBN 0-634-06918-7

HOMESPUN
Tapes

EXCLUSIVELY DISTRIBUTED BY

HAL•LEONARD®
CORPORATION

7777 W. BLUEMOUND RD. P.O. BOX 13819 MILWAUKEE, WI 53213

Visit Hal Leonard Online at
www.halleonard.com

Artie Traum
Essential Blues for Acoustic Guitar

Introduction

Essential Blues for Acoustic Guitar is designed to help you quickly become a better blues player. I recorded it as though I were sitting down and showing ideas to a friend. It's an informal lesson, full of riffs, chords, and bass lines that I play all the time. I decided to cover blues with a flatpick as well as fingerstyle. Both techniques are essential to being a good player, and I heartily recommend learning to play both ways. Using a flatpick has its own set of challenges—it may take a while to get used to controlling the pick.

To me, good musicianship is synonymous with control and timing. Learn to control your flatpick and your fingers and keep a steady beat going. I suggest working with a click-track or a metronome to keep your tempos honest. Everyone slows down and speeds up. A metronome gives you a way to self-adjust and return to the BPM (beats per minute) where you started the song.

If you're familiar with basic chords and know a little about the fingerboard you'll find lots of helpful information here. You don't have to suffer to play the blues, but you will have to practice! And I think it's very important to know about the history of the blues, where it comes from, and how the tradition developed and evolved over the past 100 years.

A Few Comments About Blues History

I feel extremely lucky to live in a time when CDs, the internet, and DVDs are a normal part of our lives. By merely clicking on a button, we can scan through thousands of songs, guitar chords, and fingerpicking tablature. I occasionally have to pinch myself and remember it wasn't always easy to learn a musical style. Although we've got access to more information than we could learn in a dozen lifetimes, I sometimes wonder if musicians had more fun in the old days. The information of the blues (its DNA) was passed down verbally in those days from generation to generation—in a kind of informal apprenticeship and initiation.

If you lived in rural Mississippi in 1928 and wanted to learn to play blues guitar you'd try to hook up with the best player in the area. You might have to walk 20 to 30 miles on a dirt road surrounded by miles of cotton to get to town. If you were lucky—really lucky—you might see a Saturday night performance by Charley Patton, Bukka White, Mattie Delaney, Ma Rainey ("Mother of the Blues"), or Robert Johnson. Blues artists didn't play in theaters, concert halls, or stadiums in those days; you'd have to catch them at a levee camp, on a street corner (where artists like Blind Willie McTell often performed), or at a fish-fry or barbeque.

Poverty, hunger, and discrimination were all part of life along the dusty back roads of Mississippi and East Texas in those days. Violence and intimidation were daily occurrences. Mississippi held the highest murder rate in the nation, and most working people were underpaid, under-educated, and poor. Some cities held hope for progressive change, but in the smaller towns racism held social strata and pre-Civil War traditions were still firmly in place. One exception was the city of Greenville, dubbed "The Queen City of the Delta." Greenville was a fairly sophisticated metropolis, with a vibrant music scene and dozens of clubs and restaurants. W.C. Handy could be seen playing blues piano well into the night at the Elysian Club. Blues performers were drawn to town to perform at gambling houses, juke joints, and private clubs—a few actually allowed integrated audiences.

A more backwater town with a less alluring social scene, Jackson, Mississippi also hosted a vibrant blues guitar scene. Tommy Johnson learned from blues innovators Willie Brown and Charley Patton. "He loved to teach his music to others, and virtually hundreds of musicians followed him around," accounts writer Dave Evans in the liner notes to the collection *Jackson Blues 1928-1938* on Yazoo Records. B.B. King, Muddy Waters, and Howlin' Wolf all acknowledge Charley Patton, who played in his own quirky style. After picking cotton all day, local musicians would seek out Patton. "He used to play at the plantation, at different homes," Howlin' Wolf told writer Pete Welding. "There were no clubs like nowadays."

Blues came out of the bitter poverty of the rural South and the oppression of the black community by a brutal system of land ownership, political control, and remnants of slavery. You can hear the social pain in the recordings of Blind Lemon Jefferson, who became one of the most famous blues artists of the 1920s. Jefferson's cutting lyrics and driving guitar style capture the spirit of those times. Few musicians enjoyed commercial success like Blind Lemon, but they all found relief playing music on the patchwork of plantations and farms that dotted the South. It wasn't long before the style moved up the Mississippi River and across the Appalachians to Tennessee, Virginia, the Piedmont, and up to Chicago.

All guitar playing was acoustic before the electric guitar was invented, and many guitars were makeshift contraptions played by calloused hands strumming across rusted strings. Some musicians worked in the cotton fields during the day and played blues at night. We know about Muddy Waters, Howlin' Wolf, and Son House, but most bluesmen were never recorded. We don't know their names, their faces, or what they sounded like. We know there were hundreds of unknown people playing and singing the blues (sometimes just singing and hollerin' in the fields), and in their isolation they created endless variations and styles of blues. Charley Patton's style was vastly different from that developed by Washington "Booker" White, which is equally different from Mae Glover.

Perhaps it's because many of the blues players lived and worked on enormous Delta plantations—isolated from other musicians—that each one developed his or her unique sound. They only met one another during trips to the city or by chance at parties or dances.

Some bluesmen took a risk by heading out on their own to try their luck performing on the road. They'd play on a dusty Delta corner to make a few bucks, perhaps jam with a friend, and then move on. Robert Johnson came and went somewhat mysteriously, playing at levee camps and juke joints. Johnny Shines described him as a "peculiar fellow," which is a bit of an understatement. Johnson had been a tenacious student. He'd sneak out of his house at night to watch Son House and Charley Patton, driving them half crazy by bugging them to teach him their riffs. Robert Johnson's style, preserved on just 29 recordings, is still studied today for its off-beat rhythms and driving bass lines.

In many early blues, you can hear guitarists trying to capture the piano riffs of Jimmy Yancey and Pine Top Smith and making them work on guitar. As blues became codified and structured, "Twelve-Bar Blues" or "Sixteen-Bar Blues" became a standard form that everyone in a band could follow. Rufus Thomas once called 12-bar blues the "backbone of American music." But you only need to listen to Skip James or Texas' Lightnin' Hopkins to hear that solo musicians crept across bar lines more often than not.

I don't want to give the impression that the blues is a Mississippi invention. Blues has deep roots in East Texas, Arkansas, Tennessee, Georgia, and Louisiana. St. Louis produced a unique crop of blues guitarists, including the little-known Charley Jordan who played "Spoonful Blues" in the distinctive thumping style of Leadbelly. There are many more blues players to explore and literally dozens of re-issue recordings worth a listen.

In the 1940s, during the black migration, an era when sharecroppers and farmers migrated to Chicago and Detroit in search of higher-paying industrial jobs, the blues followed the same route. Where Delta blues was raw and uninhibited, an even gutsier electric blues emerged from the urban landscape. In New York, Boston, and Washington D.C., the blues took on a sophistication in the hands of Josh White, Brownie McGhee, and Big Bill Broonzy, but much traditional blues was reborn as an electric style. Rock 'n' roll comes out of the blues, as does some country music.

To be a good blues guitarist, you have to know the tradition. It doesn't cut it to just pick up a guitar, play some riffs, and scrunch up your face like B.B. King. It requires homework—listening to CDs, reading, studying, and if possible visiting places like the Rock 'n' Roll Hall of Fame in Cleveland, the Experience Music Project in Seattle, or the blues museums in Mississippi. There are a gazillion CDs and books. I recommend Peter Guralnick's *Lost Highway, The Legacy of the Blues* by Sam Charters, and Alan Lomax's *The Land Where the Blues Began*—all excellent source materials.

Houston-born Lightnin' Hopkins is at the top of my list of essential blues players. He used walking bass lines and unexpected rhythms on the treble strings, punctuated by bending strings and tremolo—not unlike John Lee Hooker. Check out his slightly behind-the-beat vocal phrasing—a deep confident voice offset by driving guitar work—on "Baby Please Don't Go."

Skip James remains one of my favorites, playing often in open G minor tuning. His "Devil Got My Woman" is the ultimate fingerstyle blues, with rapid-moving syncopation in the right hand and haunting, unresolved chords. If you don't know Skip James, you probably do know his song "I'm So Glad," which the band Cream made famous.

The list of touring blues musicians you can see today includes Guy Davis, Clarence "Gatemouth" Brown, John Hammond, Jr., Taj Mahal, Bonnie Raitt, John Cephas, Paul Geremia, Eric Bibb, Kelly Joe Phelps, Sonny Landreth, Jorma Kaukonen, Rory Block, and dozens more. That acoustic blues is now performed by men and women, black, white, Japanese, and Italian musicians is testament to the enduring appeal of the music. Yet there's no denying that blues is an African-American invention, and this powerful community will always remain the copyright holders of this living tradition.

Flatpick or Fingerpicks?

Whether you decide to use a flatpick or fingerpicks, or just play with your bare fingers, well, it's your choice. In order to make that choice, you need to try playing each way. Ultimately you'll feel what's right for you. Albert King used his thumb to play, as did jazz guitarist Wes Montgomery. The vast majority of lead blues players use a flatpick, especially to enhance the attack on single strings. Flatpicks were once made of tortoise shell; now, however, they're made of plastic, which saves an endangered species from further harm and destruction. I suggest trying a hard pick and a soft pick. Hard picks will increase your attack and allow for louder, punchier notes. Soft picks can be easier to control and produce a sweeter, gentle sound.

Blues Turnarounds

When you get to the end of a blues progression, you've got to find a way to start over again. This is the purpose of the blues turnaround—to get you back to the first measure. Technically, it occurs in the last two measures of a blues and is a series of notes or chords that sets up the next verse. Turnarounds can be very simple or quite complex, depending on the player and what he or she wants to achieve between verses. I've included a number of turnarounds on this program, since they often double as phrases that can be used to create solos.

Pentatonic Blues Scale and Bending Notes

There are many books and videos that address the idea of pentatonic blues scales. I touch upon this scale briefly to get you familiar with note choices for soloing and lead lines. To play great lead lines, you've got to know about vibrato, bending strings, and tremolo. In the old days players like B.B. King would bend strings to approximate the sound of bottleneck (slide) style. "I learned to trill my finger," he once said. The combination of pushing the string up a half or whole step (generally on the 3rd, 2nd, or 1st strings) and adding vibrato (by moving the finger briskly on the fretted string) will give you a true blues sound. As I mention, try lining up three fingers on a string (1st, 2nd, and 3rd usually) *before* bending it up. For the most part your fingers will line up on the scale tone *below* the note you're bending to. The combined strength of these fingers will give you extra power. Come on strings, make my day.

Artie Traum
Bearsville, NY

Country Boy Blues with Lead Guitar

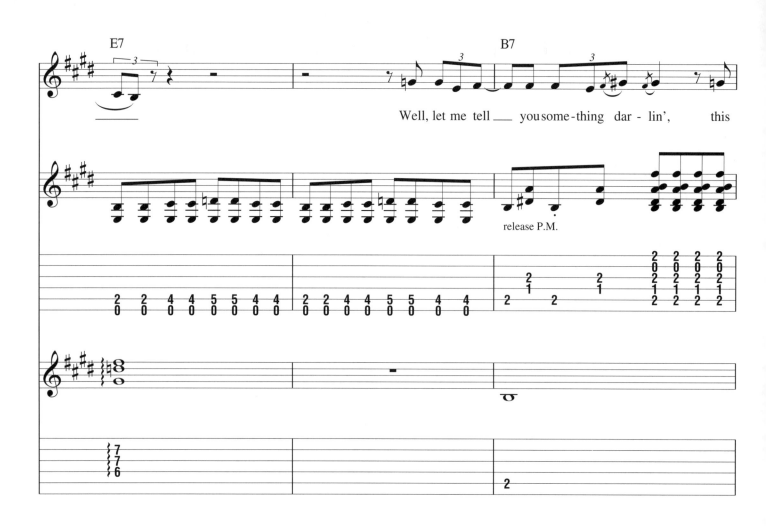

Well, let me tell ___ you some-thing dar - lin', this

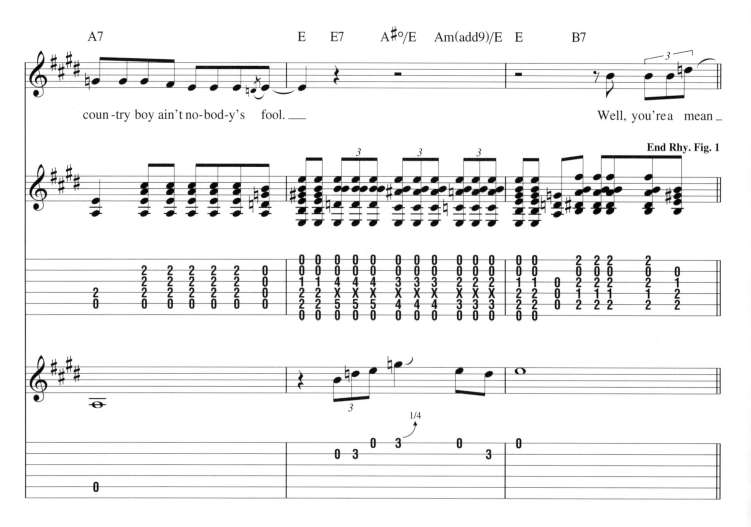

coun-try boy ain't no-bod-y's fool. ___

Well, you're a mean ___

End Rhy. Fig. 1

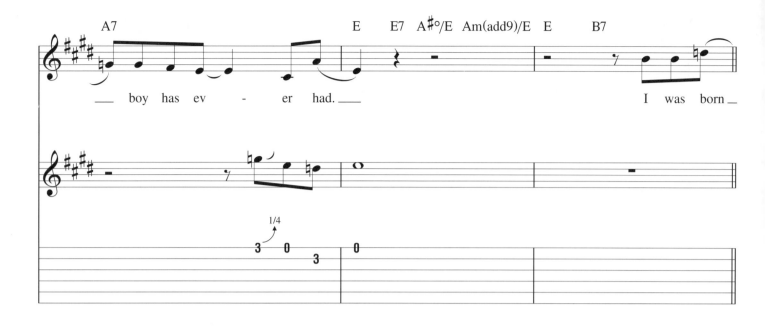

boy has ev - er had. ___ I was born ___

Verse

Gtr. 1: w/ Rhy. Fig. 1, *sim.*

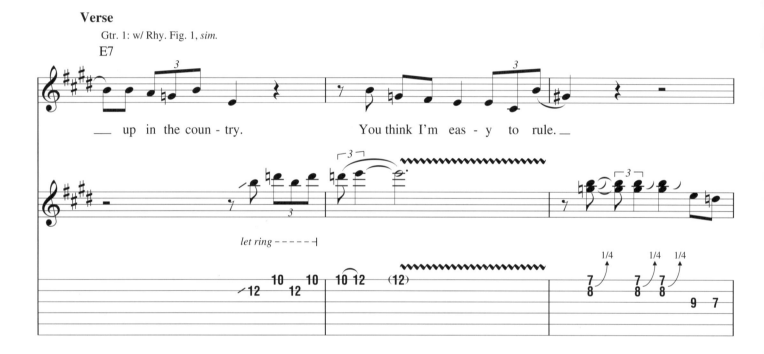

___ up in the coun - try. You think I'm eas - y to rule. ___

let ring - - - - -|

Well, I was born ___ in - to the coun - try. You think I'm eas - y to rule. ___

grad. release

* Sung as even eighth notes.

10

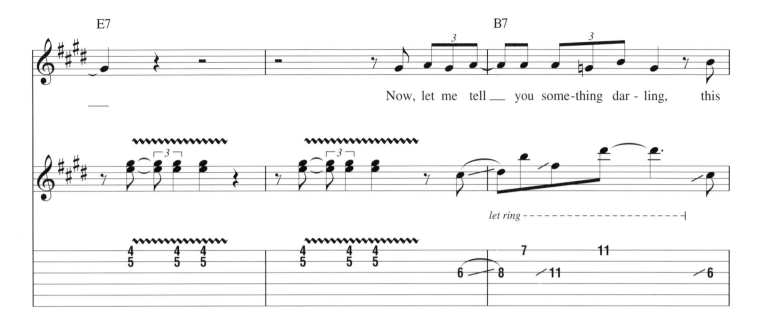

Now, let me tell ___ you some-thing dar - ling, this

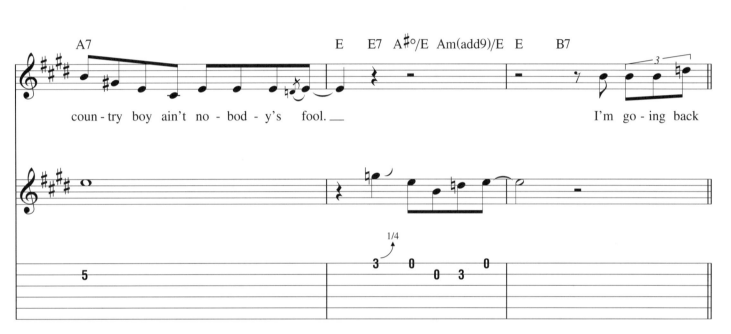

coun - try boy ain't no - bod - y's fool. ___

I'm go - ing back

Verse

Gtr. 1: w/ Rhy. Fig. 1, *sim.*

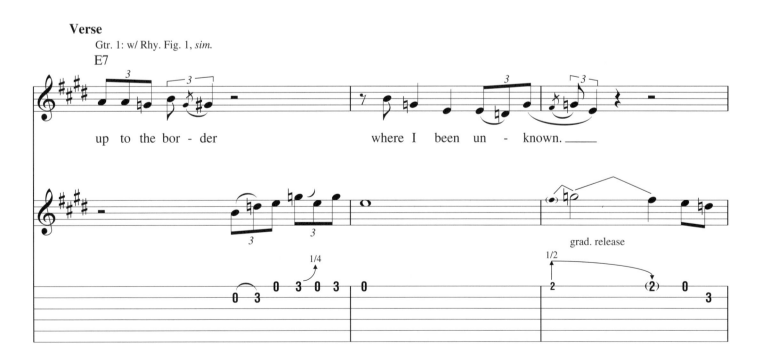

up to the bor - der

where I been un - known. ___

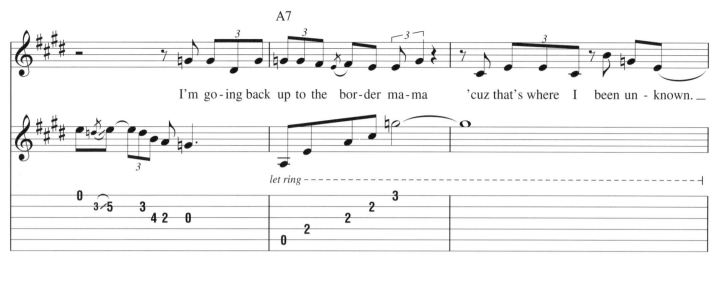

I'm go-ing back up to the bor-der ma-ma 'cuz that's where I been un-known.

All these coun-try boy — wom-en won't

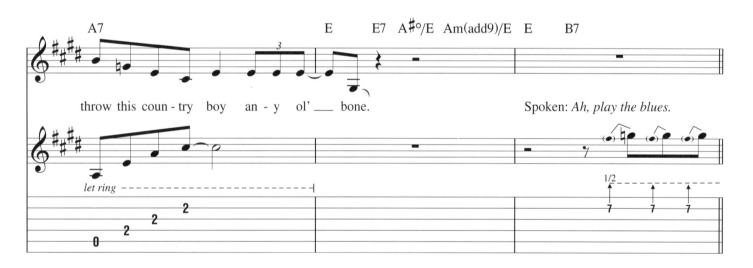

throw this coun-try boy an-y ol' — bone.

Spoken: *Ah, play the blues.*

Guitar Solo

Gtr. 1: w/ Rhy. Fig. 1 (1st 8 meas.)

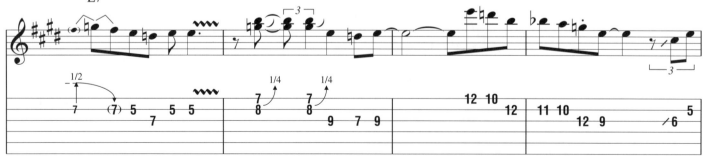

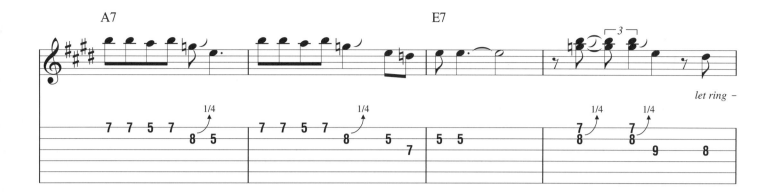

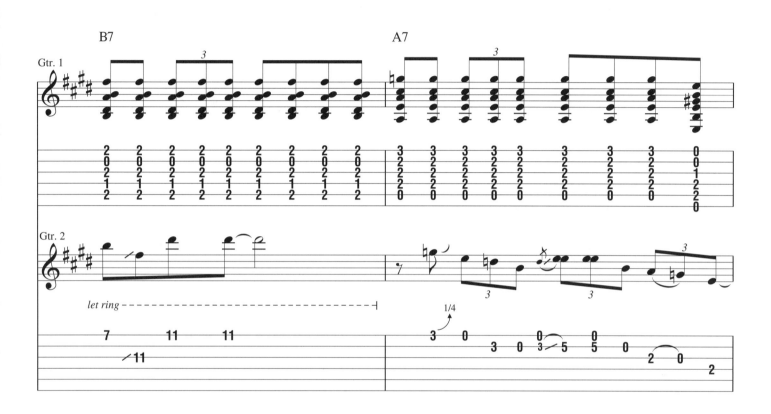

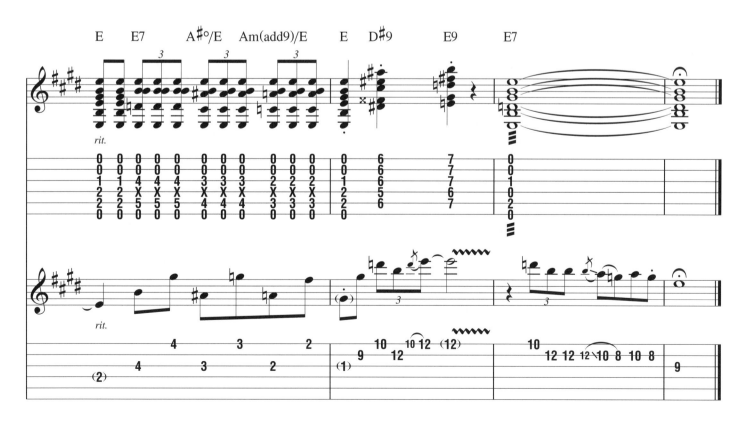

Tune Up

Track 2   Standard Tuning: E-A-D-G-B-E

Bass Note Rhythm Patterns

Track 3

Example 1

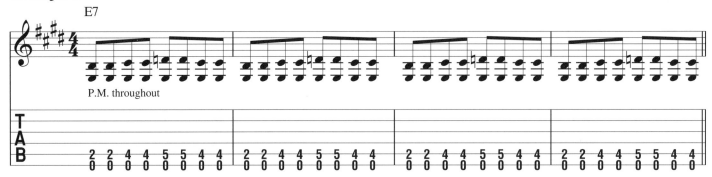

Example 2

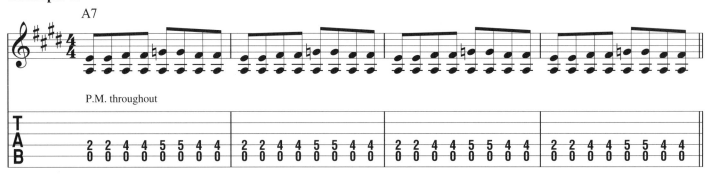

Example 3

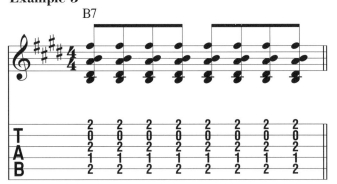

Example 4

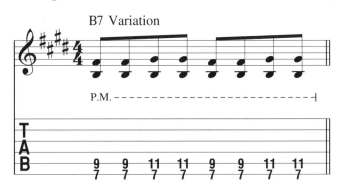

Example 5

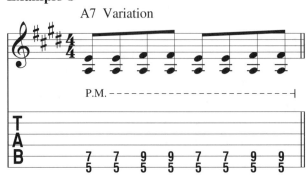

Complete Bass Note Rhythm–12 Bar Blues

Track 4

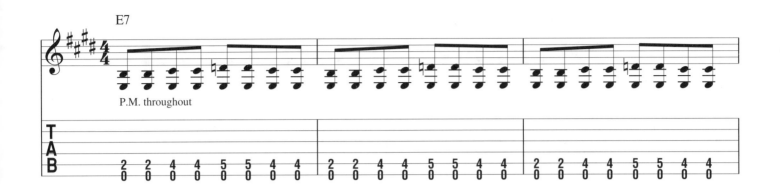

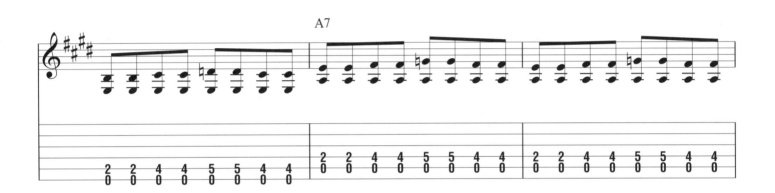

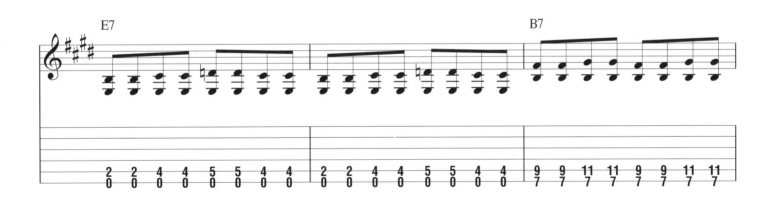

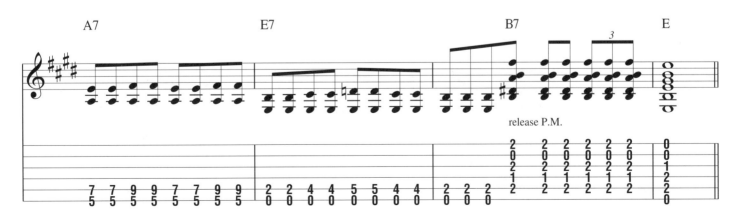

Country Boy Blues–Key of A

Track 5

Example 1

Example 2

Example 3

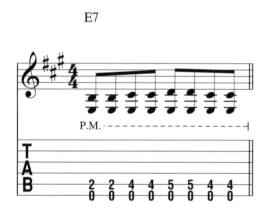

Example 4 Ending
(Insert at measure 11)

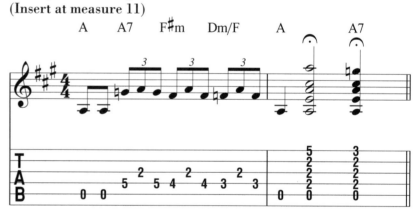

 ## Bass Note Rhythms–Other Keys

Track 6

Example 1

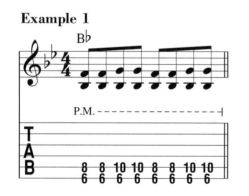

Example 2

Example 3

Turnarounds–Key of E

Track 7

Example 1
(Insert at measure 11)

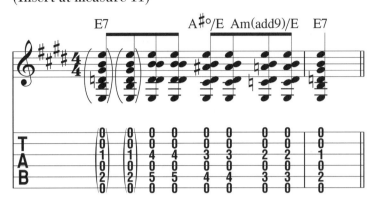

Example 2

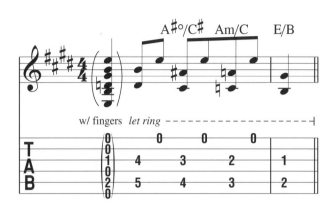

Example 3

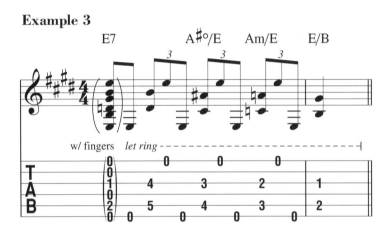

Example 4

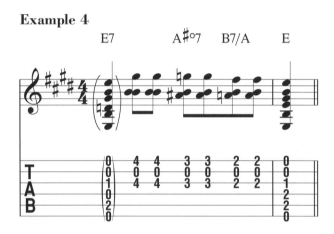

Example 5

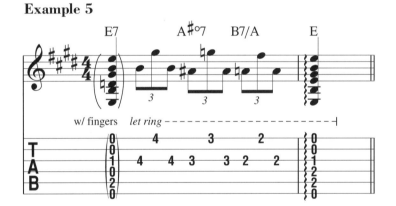

Example 6

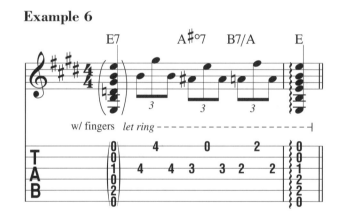

Example 7

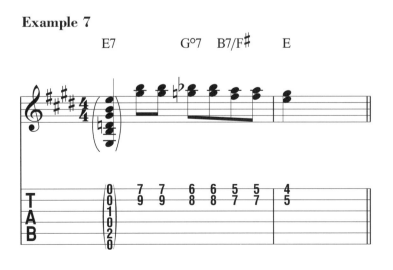

Example 8

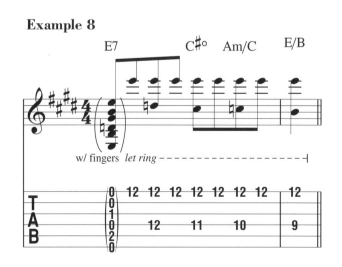

Example 9

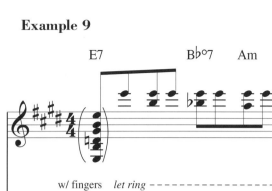

Example 10

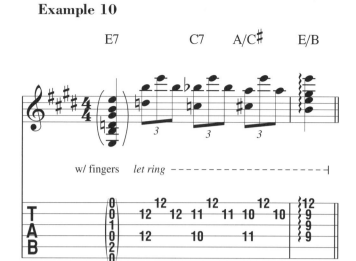

 Lightnin' Hopkins Blues Riff

Track 8

Example 1

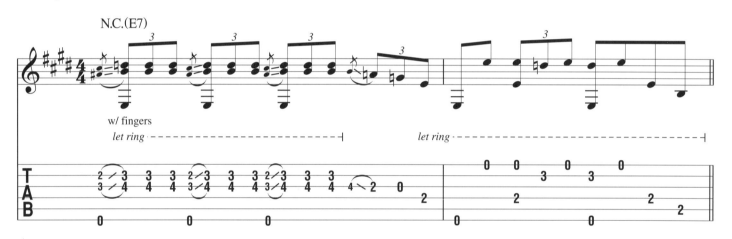

Example 2
Variation on 1st Measure

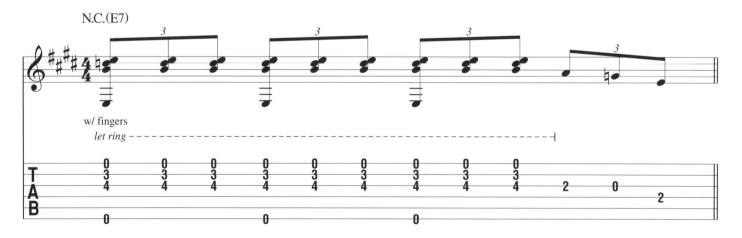

Example 3
Full 12-Bar Blues with Lightnin' Hopkins Riff

Track 9

Come Back Baby–Fingerstyle

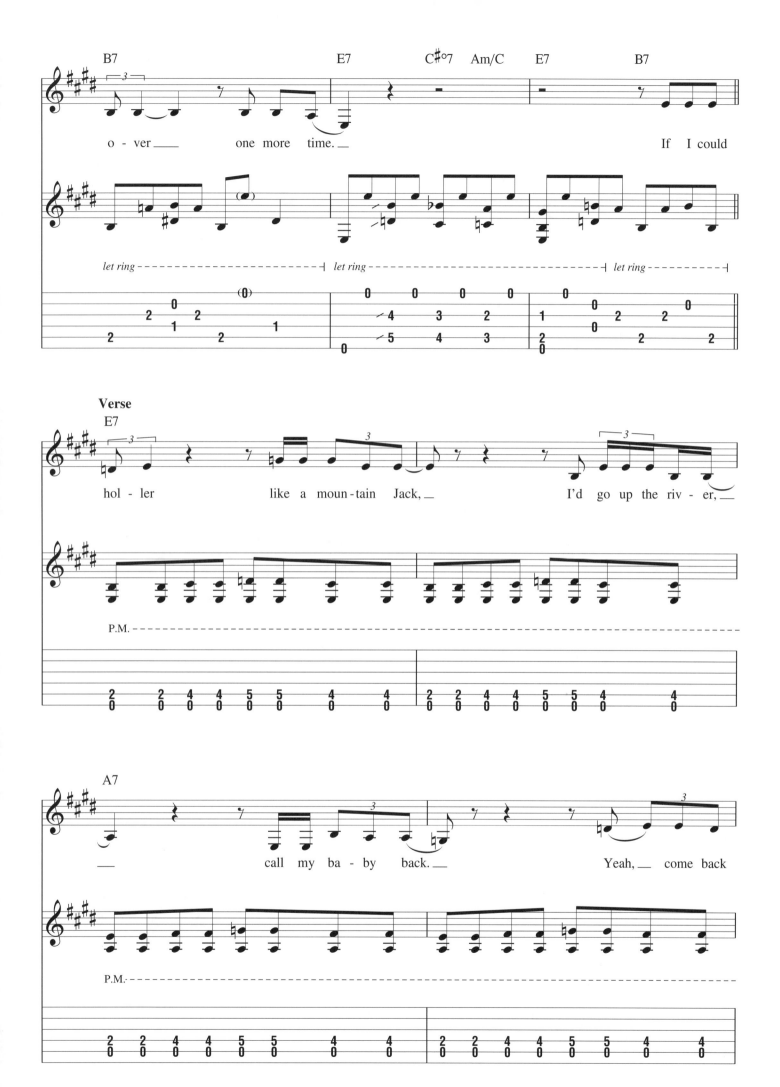

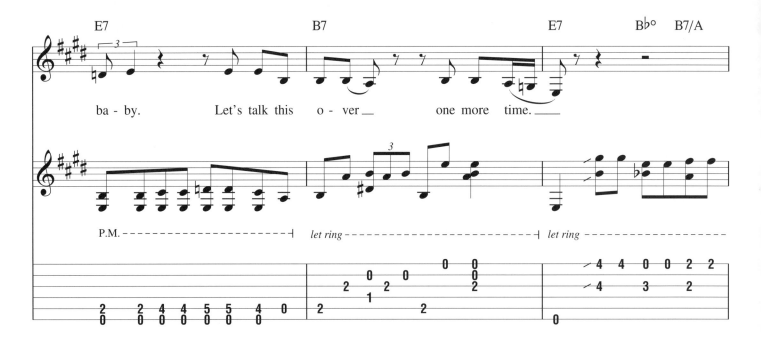

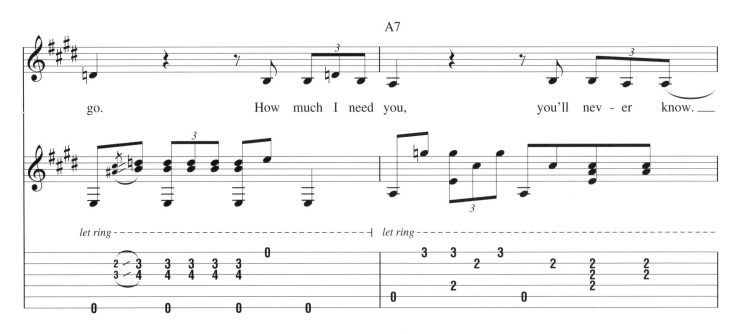

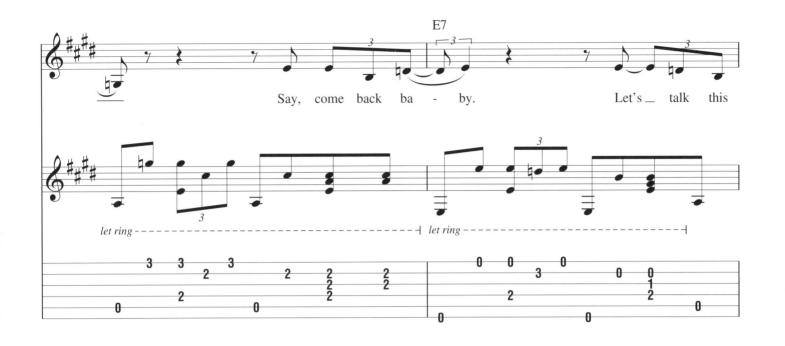

Say, come back ba - by. Let's __ talk this

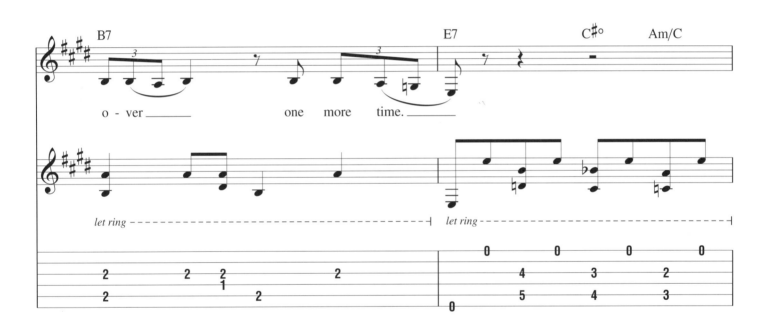

o - ver _____ one more time. _____

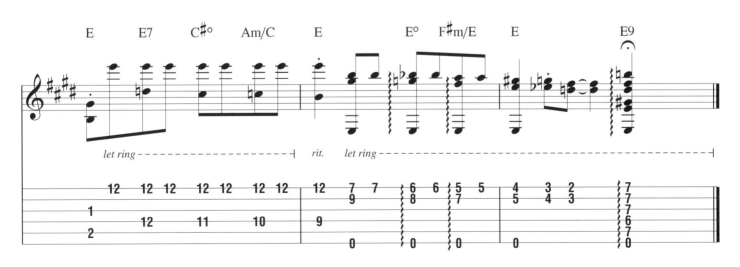

Example 1
Key of A

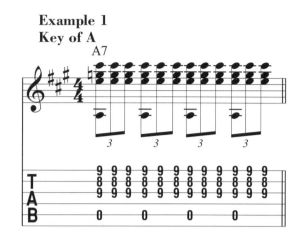

Example 2

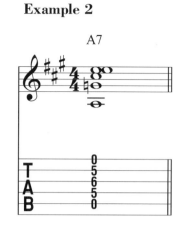

Example 3

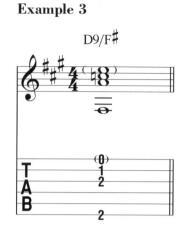

 Come Back Baby–Key of A

Track 10

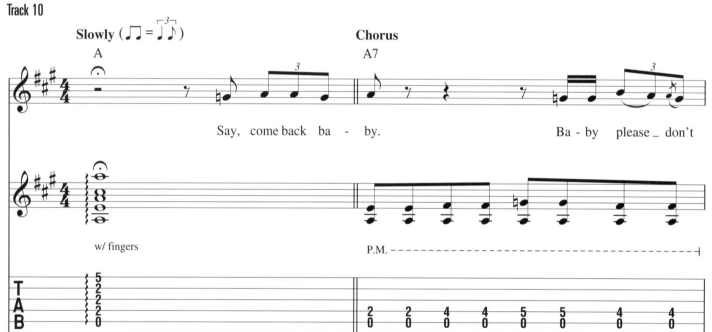

Slowly (♫ = ♪♪)

A

Chorus

A7

Say, come back ba - by. Ba - by please _ don't

w/ fingers

P.M.

D7/F#

go. How much I need you, you'll nev - er know. _

let ring

let ring

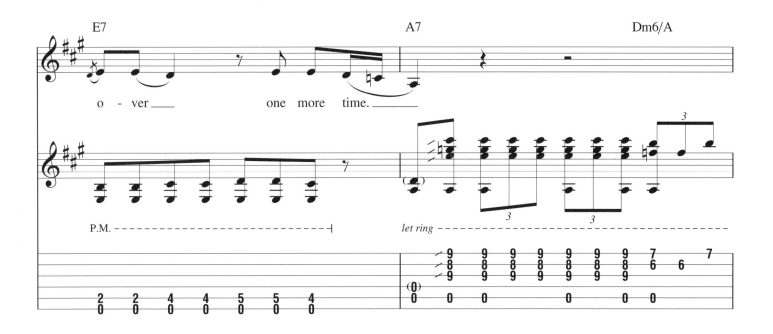

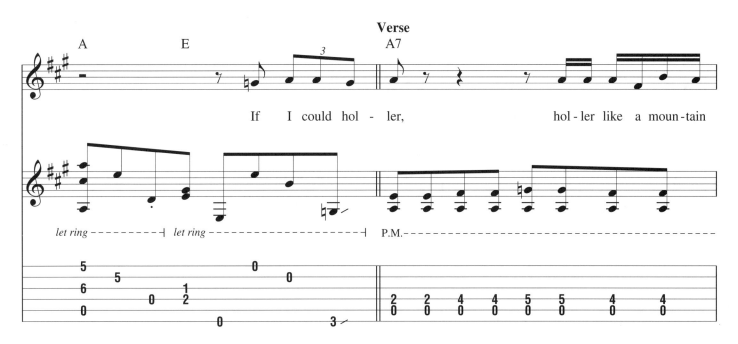

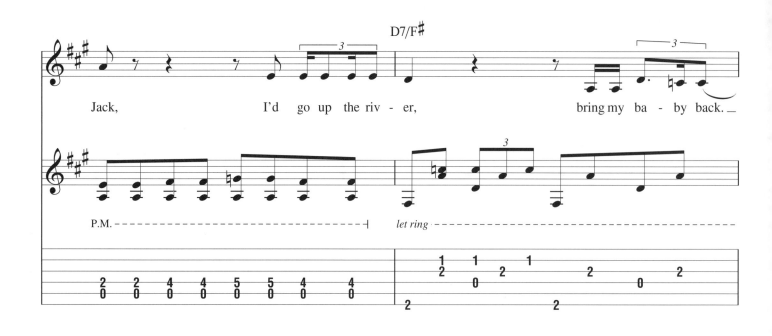

Jack, I'd go up the riv - er, bring my ba - by back.

Well, come back ba - by. Let's talk this

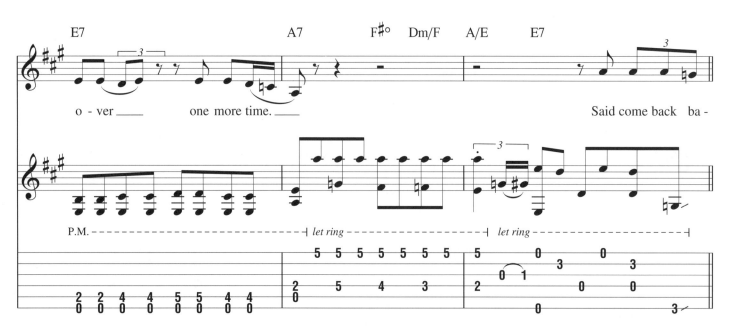

o - ver ____ one more time. ____ Said come back ba -

Chorus

by.　　　　　Ba - by please ___ don't go.　　　　How much I need ___

___ you,　　　you'll nev-er know.　　　Come back ba - by.　　　Let's talk this

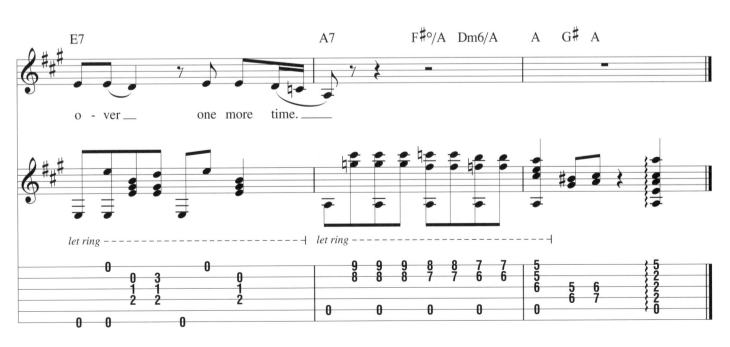

o - ver ___　　one more time. ___

Example 1

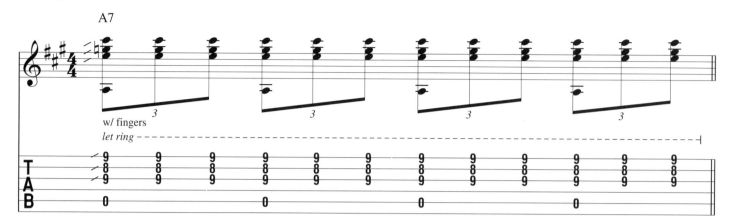

Example 2

Example 3
Fifth Position–Where Leads in A Are Based

Example 4
Turnaround in A

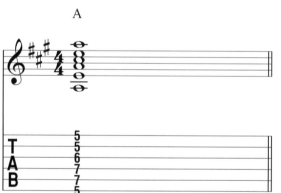

 Playing with Friends

Track 11
Example 1
A Minor Pentatonic Scale–Fifth Position

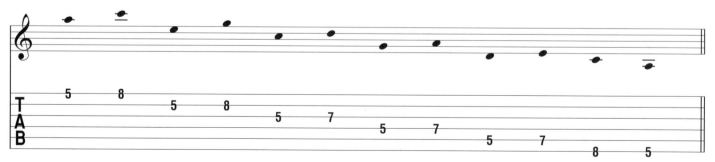

 **Lead Techniques**

Track 12

Example 1	Example 2	Example 3
Vibrato	Bending	

  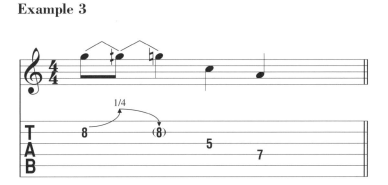

 Lead Guitar Example

Track 13

Moderately slow

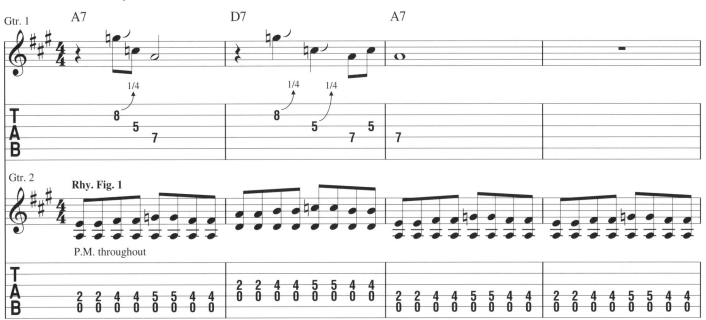

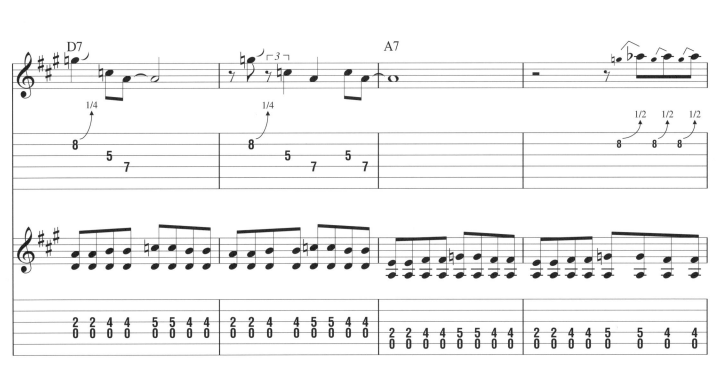

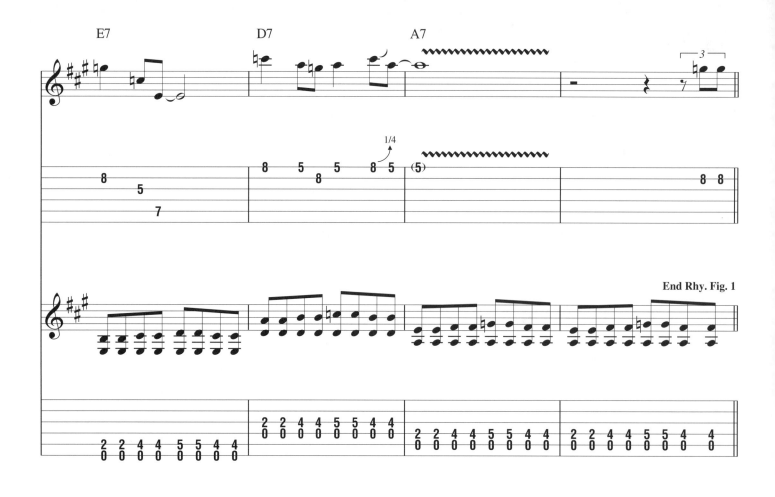

End Rhy. Fig. 1

Gtr. 2: w/ Rhy. Fig. 1 (1st 8 meas.) *sim.*

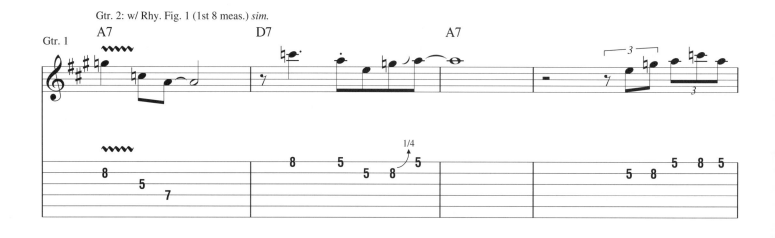

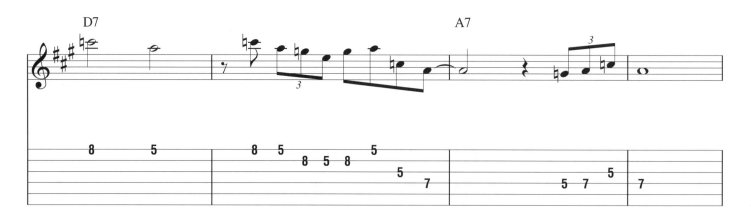

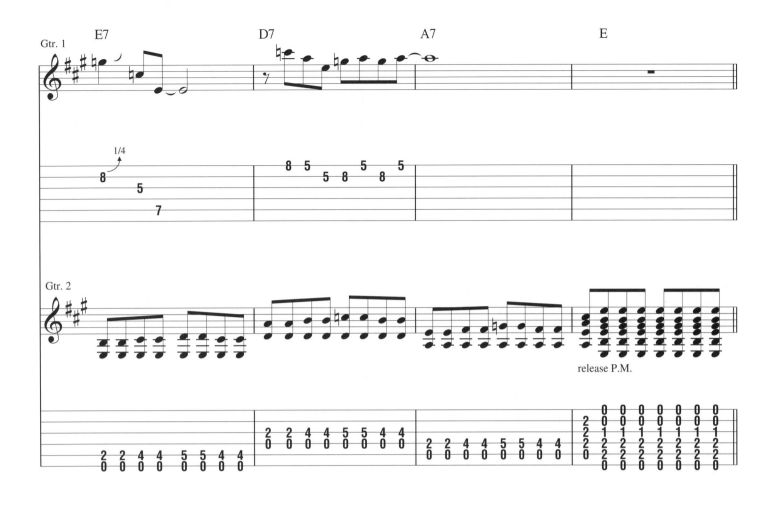

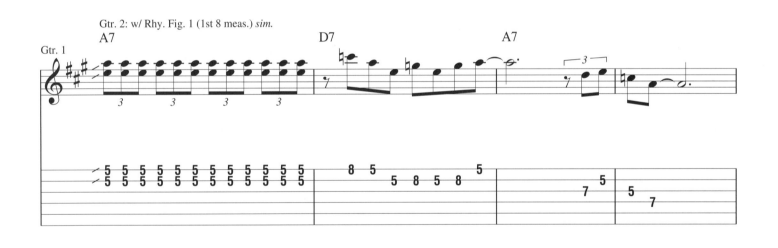

Gtr. 2: w/ Rhy. Fig. 1 (1st 8 meas.) *sim.*

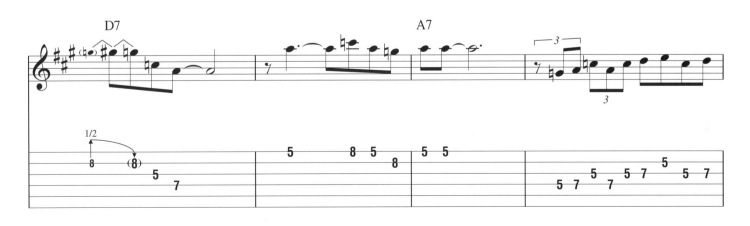

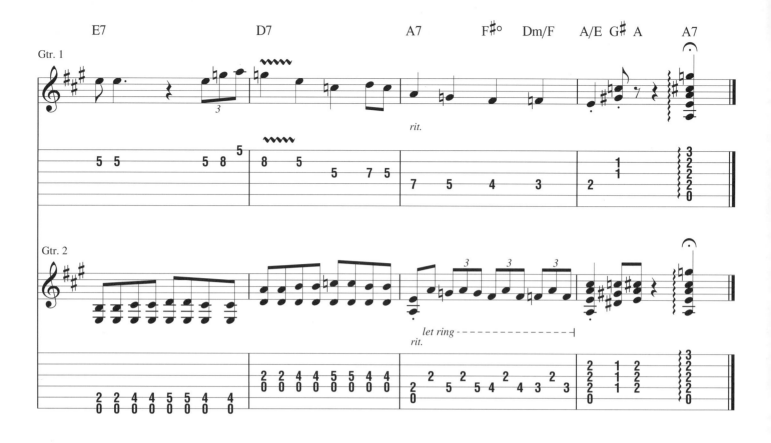

Example 1

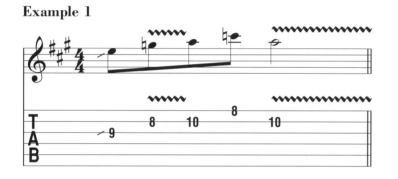

Example 2

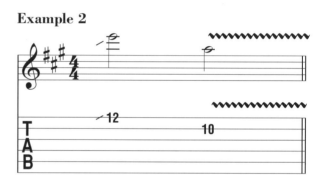

Example 3

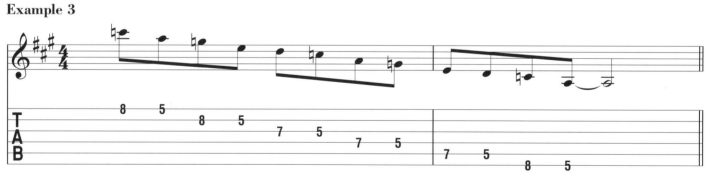

Example 4

Example 5

Example 6

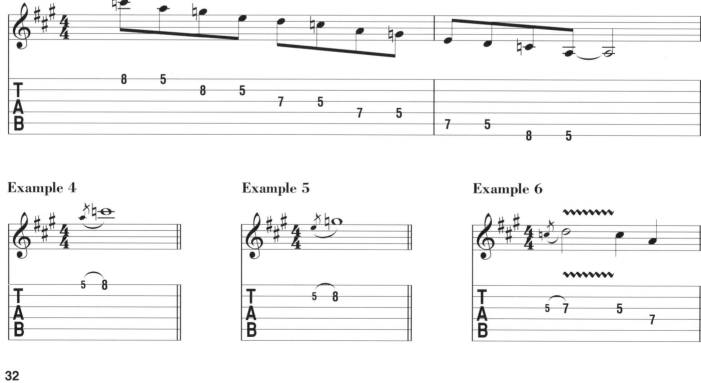

Lead Guitar Example–Faster

Track 14

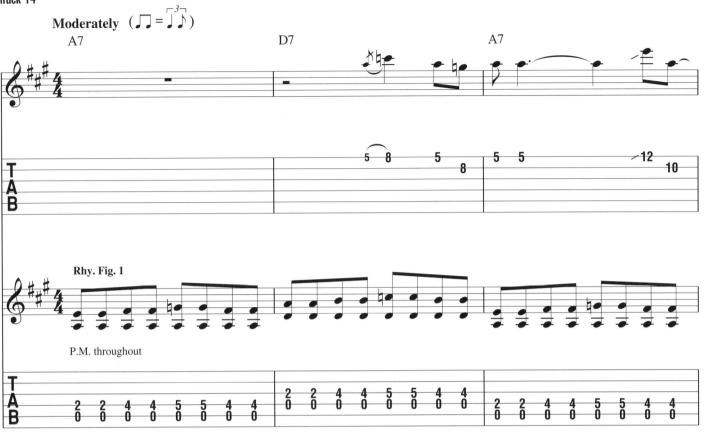

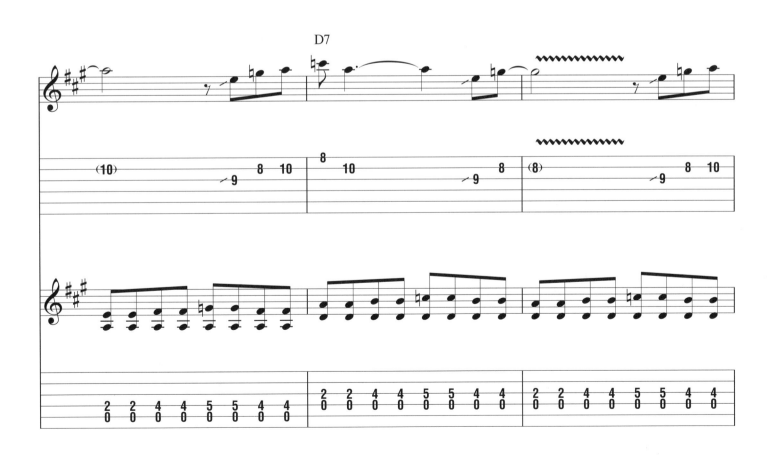

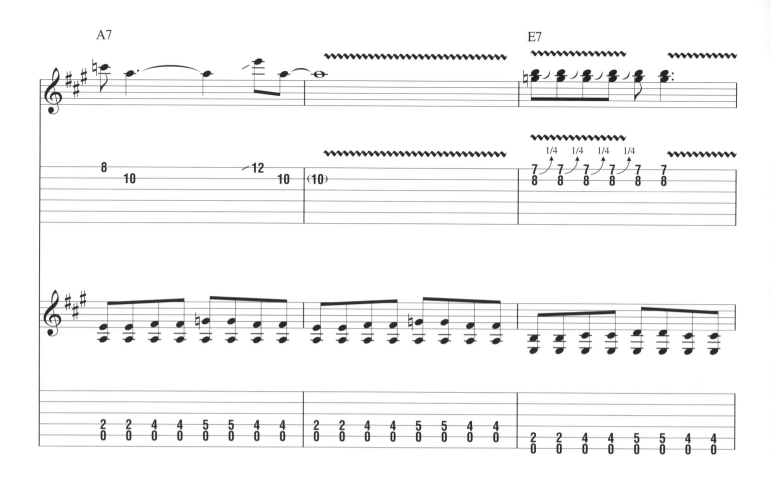

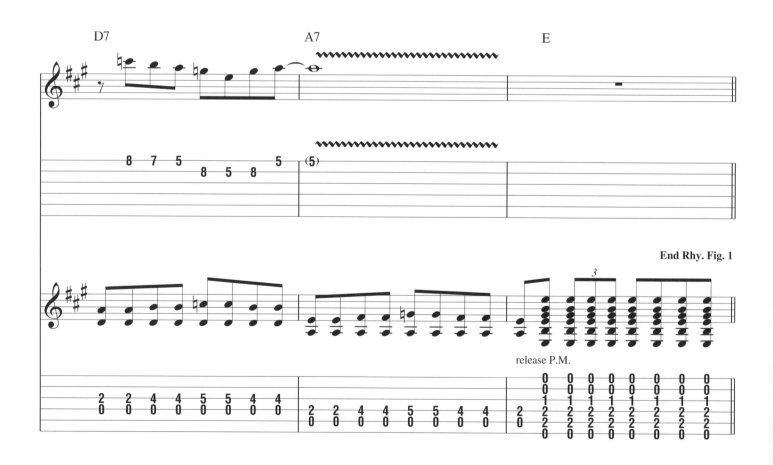

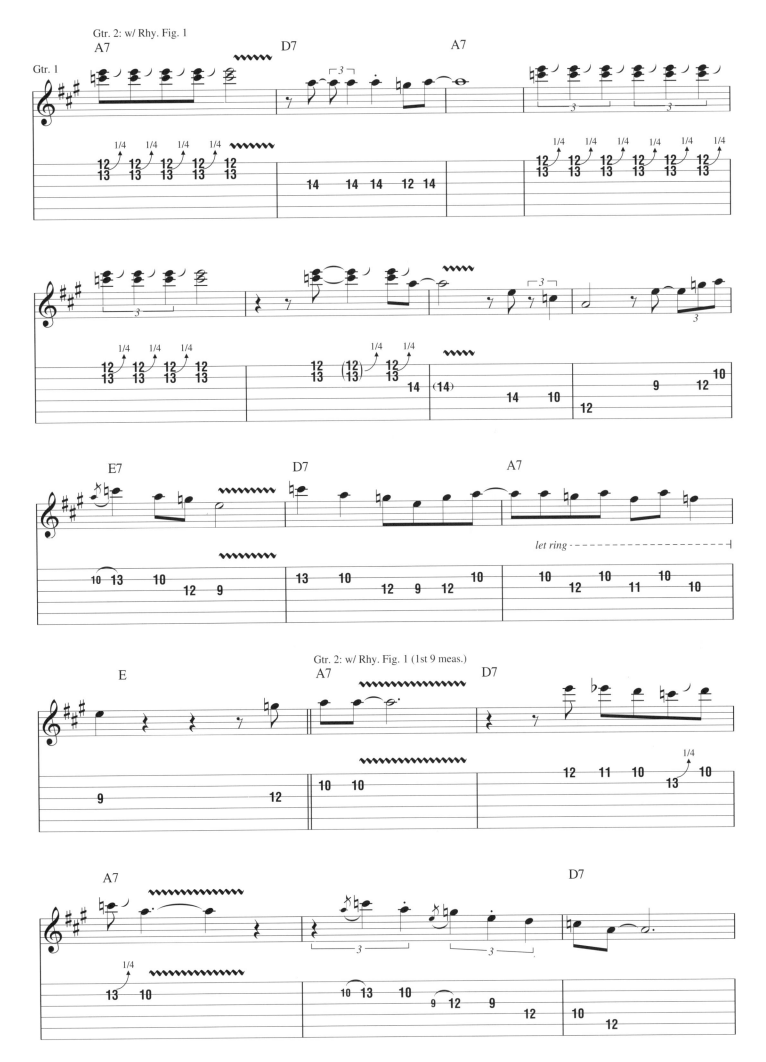

Example 1

Example 2

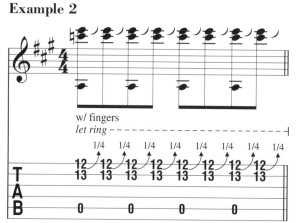

Example 3

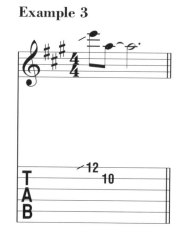

 Double-Note Bend–Key of E

Track 15

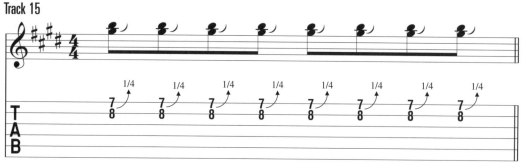

Trouble in Mind

Track 16

Chorus

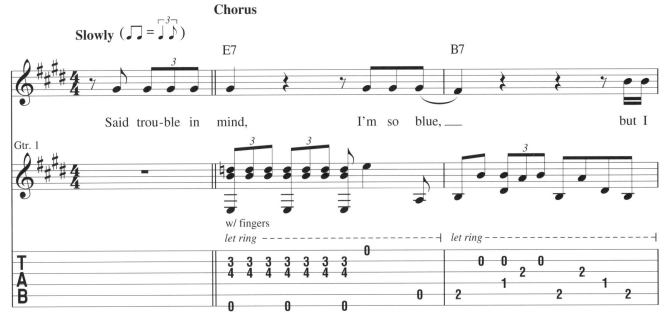

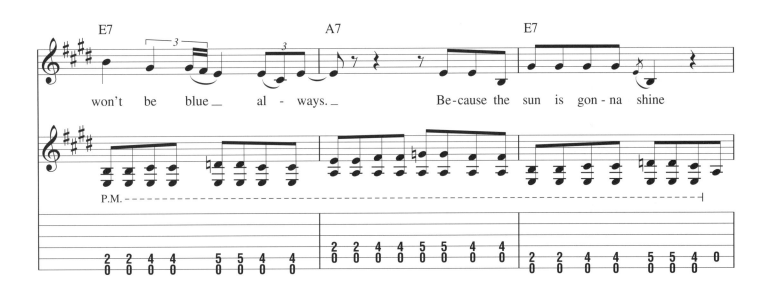

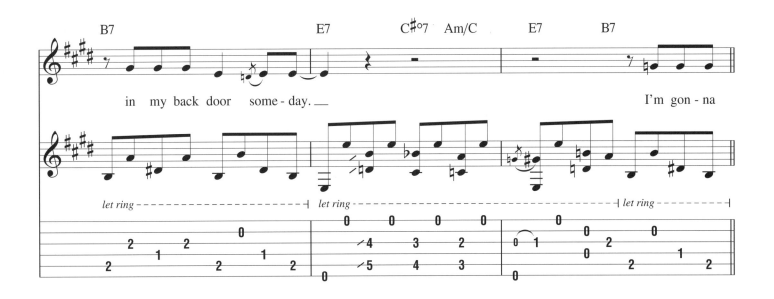

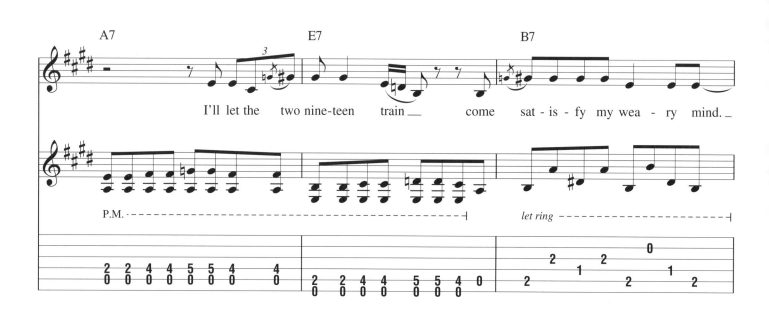

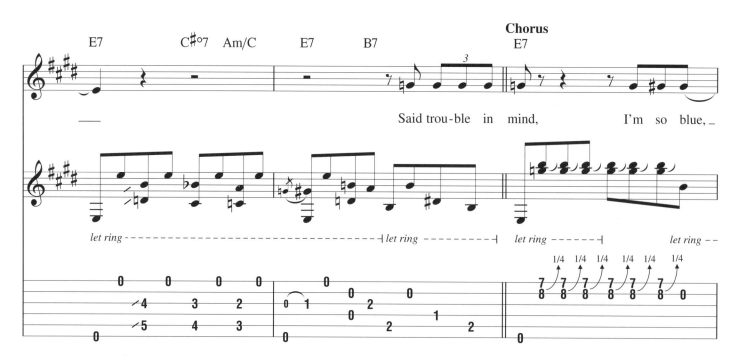

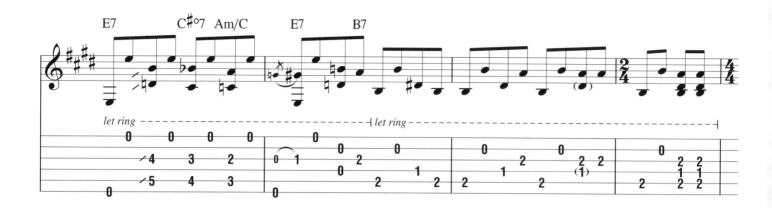

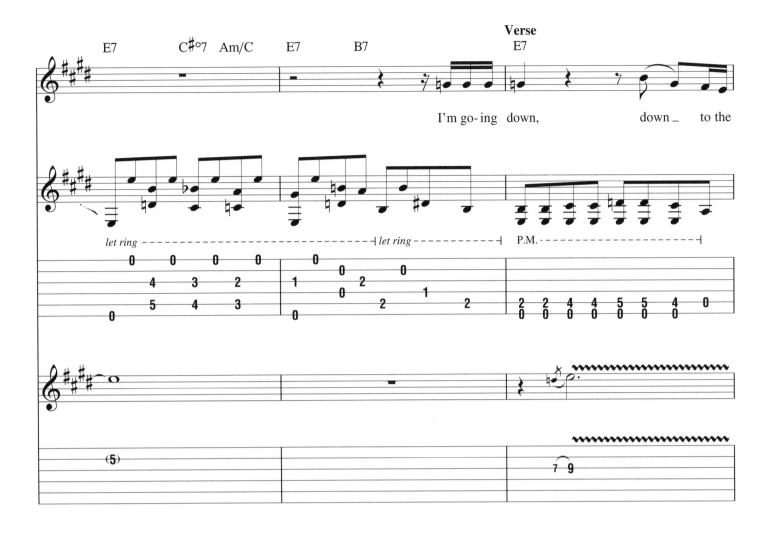

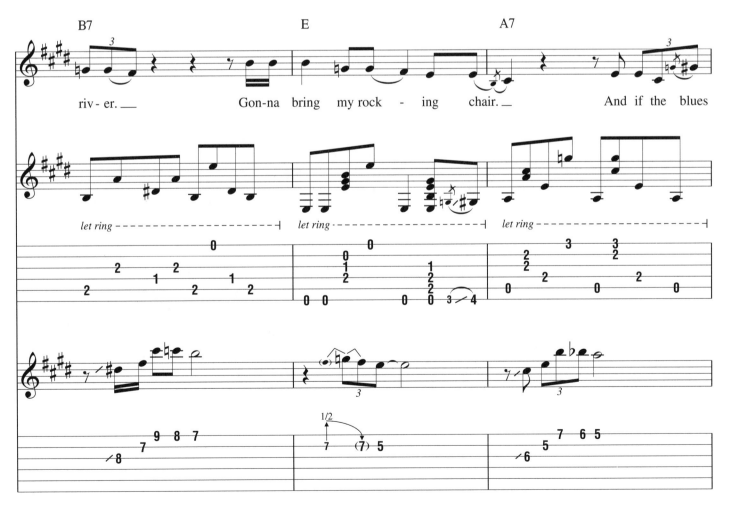

don't get me dar - lin', I walk my - self a - way from here. ___

Chorus

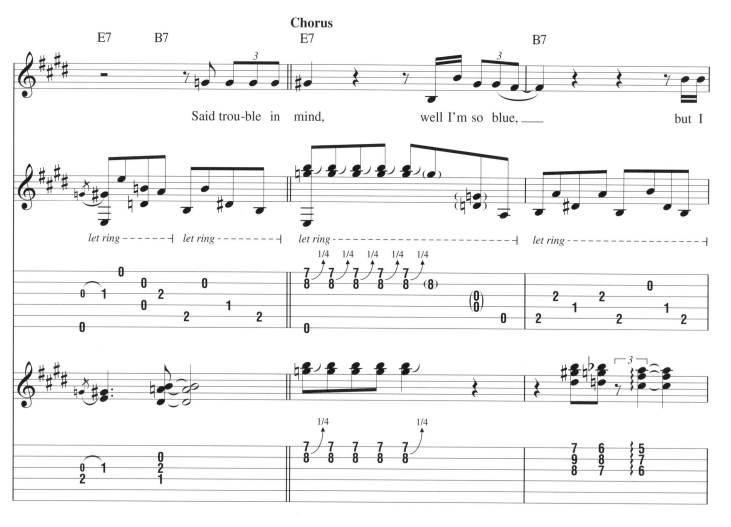

Said trou - ble in mind, well I'm so blue, ___ but I

won't be blue _ al - ways. _   Be-cause the sun is gon-na shine _

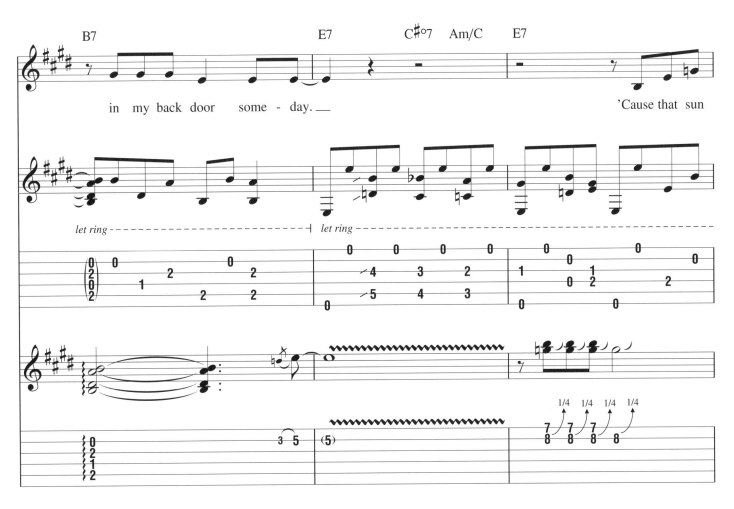

in my back door   some - day. _   'Cause that sun

is gon - na shine _____ in my back door some - day. _____

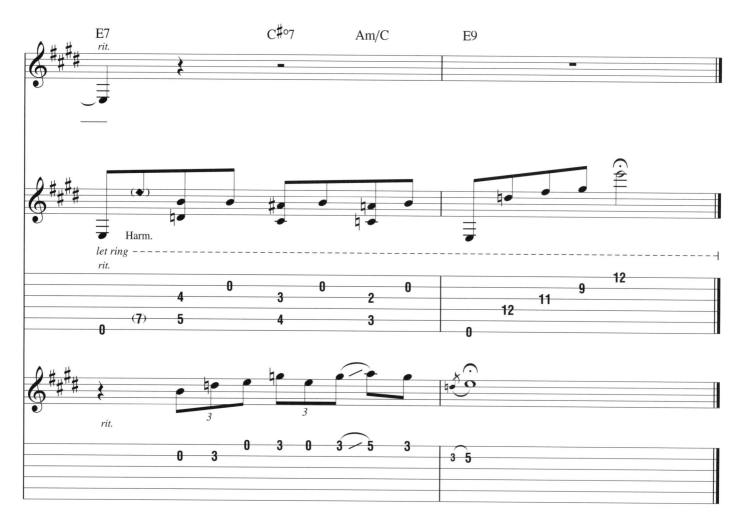

Example 1
Trouble in Mind Chord Progression

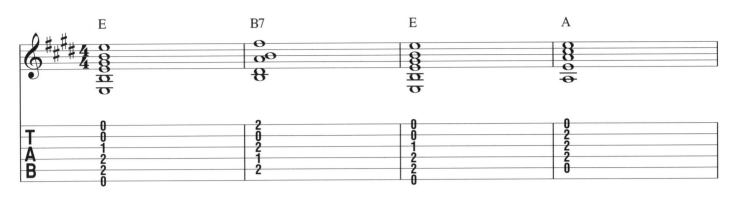

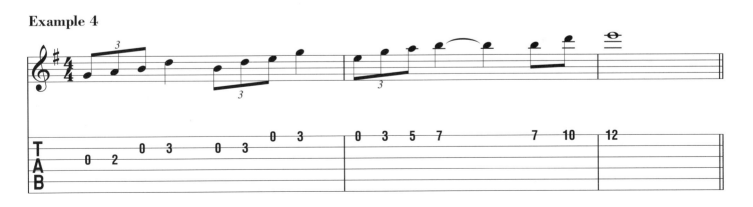

Example 2
E Minor Pentatonic Scale

Example 3

Example 4

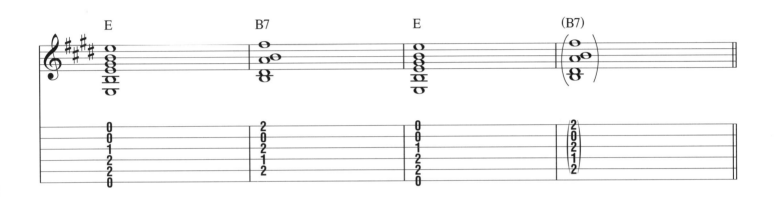

Example 5
E Minor Pentatonic Scale–Alternate Fingering

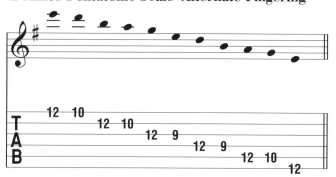

Example 6

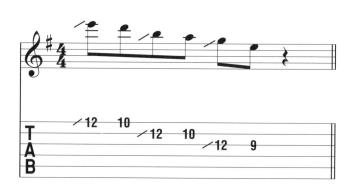

Example 7

Example 8

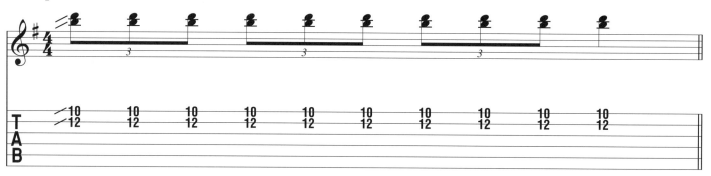

Example 9

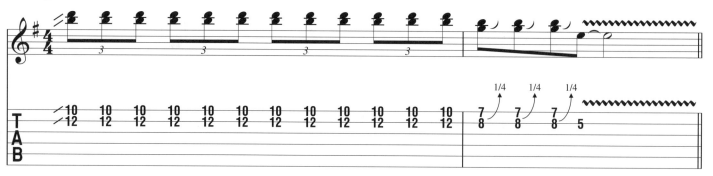

Example 10
Twelfth Position E Chord and E Minor Pentatonic Scale

Example 11

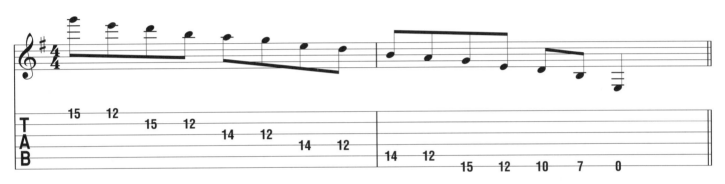

Example 12

Example 13

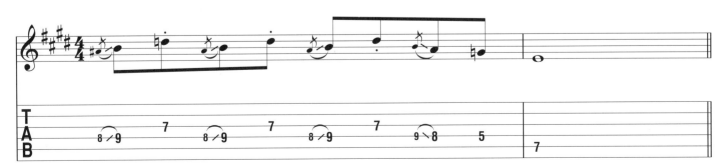

Example 14
Trouble in Mind–Fingerstyle

Said trou-ble in mind, I'm so blue, __ but I

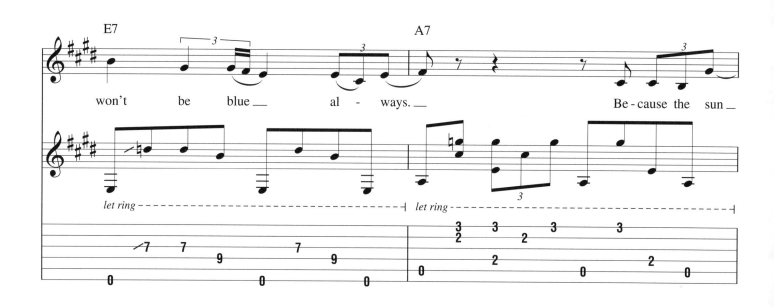

won't be blue __ al - ways. __ Be - cause the sun __

__ is gon-na shine __ in my back door some - day. __

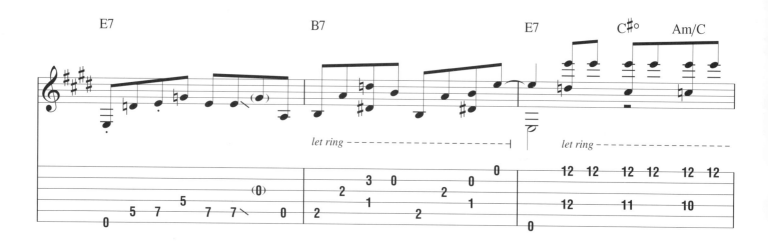

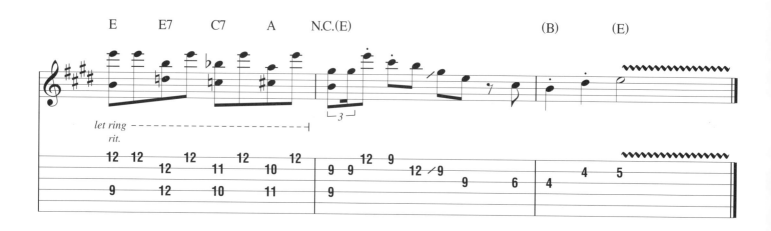

Example 15
Elmore James Riff in A

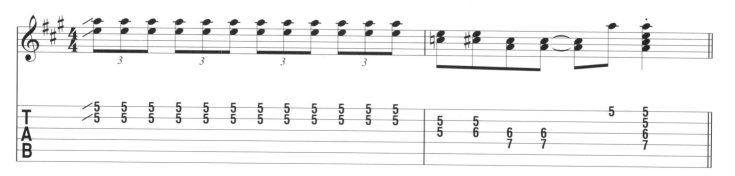

Farewell Blues in A

Track 17

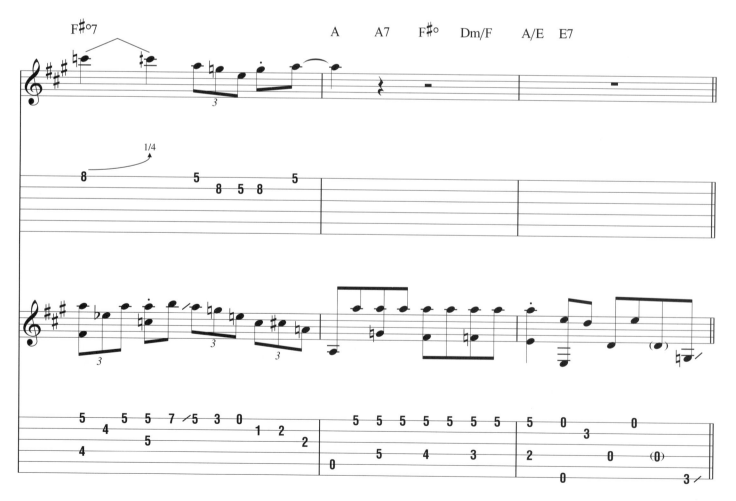

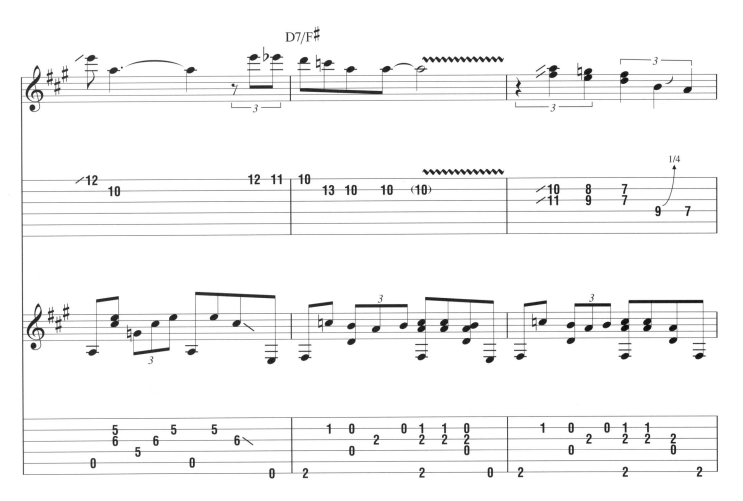

LISTEN & LEARN SERIES

This exciting new series features lessons from the top pros with in-depth CD instruction and thorough accompanying book.

GUITAR

**Russ Barenberg Teaches
Twenty Bluegrass Guitar Solos**
00695220 Book/CD Pack $19.95

**Keola Beamer Teaches
Hawaiian Slack Key Guitar**
00695338 Book/CD Pack $19.95

**Rory Block Teaches
Classics of Country Blues Guitar**
00699065 Book/CD Pack $19.95

**Roy's Blues Book – Songs & Guitar
Arrangements of Roy Book Binder**
00695808 Book/CD Pack $19.95

**Cathy Fink and Marcy Marxer's
Kids' Guitar Songbook**
00699258 Book/CD Pack $14.95

The Guitar of Jorma Kaukonen
00695184 Book/CD Pack $19.95

Tony Rice Teaches Bluegrass Guitar
00695045 Book/CD Pack $19.95

**Artie Traum Teaches
Essential Blues for Acoustic Guitar**
00695805 Book/CD Pack $19.95

**Artie Traum Teaches Essential Chords
& Progressions for Acoustic Guitar**
00695259 Book/CD Pack $14.95

**Artie Traum Teaches
101 Essential Riffs for Acoustic Guitar**
00695260 Book/CD Pack $14.95

Happy Traum Teaches Blues Guitar
00841082 Book/CD Pack $19.95

**Richard Thompson Teaches
Traditional Guitar Instrumentals**
00841083 Book/CD Pack $19.95

BANJO

**Tony Trischka Teaches
20 Easy Banjo Solos**
00699056 Book/CD Pack $19.95

MANDOLIN

**Sam Bush Teaches
Bluegrass Mandolin Repertoire**
00695339 Book/CD Pack $19.95

HARMONICA

**Paul Butterfield Teaches
Blues Harmonica**
00699089 Book/CD Pack $19.95

**John Sebastian Teaches
Blues Harmonica**
00841074 Book/CD Pack $19.95

PIANO

**David Bennett Cohen Teaches
Blues Piano**
A Hands-On Course in Traditional Blues Piano
00841084 Volume 1 Book/CD Pack...................$19.95
00290498 Volume 2 Book/CD Pack...................$19.95

Warren Bernhardt Teaches Jazz Piano
00699062 Volume 1 Book/CD Pack.............$19.95
00699084 Volume 2 Book/CD Pack.............$19.95

Dr. John Teaches New Orleans Piano
00699090 Volume 1 Book/CD Pack.............$19.95
00699093 Volume 2 Book/CD Pack.............$19.95
00699094 Volume 3 Book/CD Pack.............$19.95

PENNYWHISTLE

**Cathal McConnell Teaches
Irish Pennywhistle**
00841081 Book/CD Pack $19.95

FOR MORE INFORMATION, SEE YOUR LOCAL MUSIC DEALER,
OR WRITE TO:

HAL•LEONARD®
CORPORATION
7777 W. BLUEMOUND RD. P.O. BOX 13819 MILWAUKEE, WI 53213

Visit Hal Leonard online at
www.halleonard.com

1203

Prices and availability subject to change without notice.